Train at Home to Become a Certified Personal/Life Coach

Train at Home to Become a Certified Personal/Life Coach

The Essential Guide to Becoming a Personal Coach in Your Spare Time...and Before You Quit Your Day Job

Michelle McGarry

Writers Club Press
New York Lincoln Shanghai

Train at Home to Become a Certified Personal/Life Coach
The Essential Guide to Becoming a Personal Coach in
Your Spare Time...and Before You Quit Your Day Job

All Rights Reserved © 2003 by Michelle McGarry

No part of this book may be reproduced or transmitted in any form or by any means, graphic, electronic, or mechanical, including photocopying, recording, taping, or by any information storage retrieval system, without the written permission of the publisher.

Writers Club Press
an imprint of iUniverse, Inc.

For information address:
iUniverse
2021 Pine Lake Road, Suite 100
Lincoln, NE 68512
www.iuniverse.com

The author does not specifically endorse or recommend any particular training program. Tuition fees and program requirements are subject to change. Verify fees and requirements with individual programs.

ISBN: 0-595-27002-6

Printed in the United States of America

To Paul and Sarah who started this whole home biz craze

Contents

Introduction 1
   FAQs about Personal Coaching
   What this Book Will Do for You
   About the Coach Training Programs

Part I: Coach Certification Programs 7
Abundant Practice: A Program for Coaches 9
Academy for Coach Training 11
ADD Coaching Academy 13
Coach Spotlight: Vivian M. Rindik, Personal Coach *15*
Advantage Coaching 17
Career Coach Institute 19
Ciris Alliance: Power Coach Network 21
Coach Spotlight: Diana Haskins, Professional Effectiveness Coach *23*
Coach for Life 24
Coach University (CoachU) 26
The Coaches Training Institute (CTI) 28
Coach Spotlight: Tracy Manyfield, Life Coach *30*
Coaching from Spirit 32
Coachville 34
College of Executive Coaching 36
Coach Spotlight: Susan Martin, Strategy Coach *38*
Comprehensive Coaching U 40
Corporate Coach University International 42

EDUCOACH—The Education Coach Training Company 44
Coach Spotlight: Heather Richardson Cameron, Educational Coach 46
Executive Coach Academy 48
Fill Your Coaching Practice 50
International Coach Academy 52
Coach Spotlight: Christopher Ashe, Whole Life Personal Coach 54
Institute for Life Coach Training...56
Kadmon Academy of Human Potential 58
Life on Purpose Institute 60
Coach Spotlight: Deborah Brown, Career Coach 62
Life Purpose Institute 64
Live Your Dream by Joyce Chapman 66
MentorCoach 68
Coach Spotlight: Barbara Garro, M.A.,
Weight Loss and Weight Management Coach 70
Optimal Functioning Institute 72
Parent as Coach Academy 74
Relationship Coaching Institute 76
Coach Spotlight: Dr. Harriet Kramer Becker
and Dr. John Becker, Relationship Coaches 78
Results Life Coaching 80

Part II: Networking Organizations 83

Part III: Recommended Resources 89

Topic Index 95

About the Author 97

Introduction

What is a personal/life coach?

A personal/life coach is someone who helps people achieve their goals and dreams. She helps her clients to define and clarify their goals in life and then works with them toward achieving the desired outcome, such as starting a business, becoming financially secure, leading a balanced life, or enjoying a successful relationship. A personal coach helps her clients set goals, manage time, stay motivated, and even build their dreams. There are many types of personal coaches, such as career coaches, life purpose coaches, and corporate coaches, with many coaches combining these specializations. In addition, personal/life coaches can also specialize in particular areas such as time management, weight loss management, parenting, relationships, small business, financial management, and more.

Is coaching a growing trend?

Absolutely. The profession of coaching is growing at a rate second only to the IT industry by some studies. It is the second largest growing consulting profession. There are thousands of personal coaches in the U.S. now, and their numbers are growing every year by 25 percent! Consider this: According to *Cool Careers for Dummies* (IDG Books, 1998), more than 46 percent of men and 40 percent of women say they are still trying to figure out the meaning and purpose in their lives. Personal coaches in a variety of specializations help to fill the need.

What do coaches earn?

Coaches earn anywhere from $50–$150 per hour or more. You set your own rates as a coach. But generally, coaches can have any number of clients who pay $100 to $1000 each—per month. Setting rates depends on your level of experience and the type of coaching you offer.

Can I work from home?

Yes. Most personal coaches are in private practice in their homes. You don't even necessarily need a separate home office to make a living as a coach. Coaching can take place over the phone and even via e-mail, so you can coach anyone where there is a telephone.

What kind of experience and education do I need to become a coach?

You don't need any one particular piece of education or experience to become a coach. Some coaches are experienced therapists already who add coaching to their practice. But you do not need to be a therapist or counselor already to become a coach. You don't even need a college degree in some cases. Depending on what kind of coach you want to be and what program you want to get certified by, you can rely on your personal experience to guide you.

Many people who seek the services of a personal coach need someone with similar experience to theirs. And people come from all walks of life to become coaches. Some people who started out in the financial industry later became financial management coaches. Experienced parents have become parenting coaches. Even retired people have become coaches. The field is open to a wide range of skills and experience. A coach training program is the main avenue for coach education. They provide solid skills in the field and provide an opportunity for certification, which gives the coach extra credibility and validation.

What will this book do for me?

This book can help get you started researching the various distance-learning coach training programs. There are many in-person coach training programs as well, but this book focuses on distance-learning programs because they can reach a larger audience. Coaching is unique in that a lot of it takes place on the telephone anyway, and as a result so does most coach training. New coach training programs emerge frequently and there are a lot of programs to research. This book eliminates the need to spend weeks searching the Internet for the right program for you. It provides:

Profiles of Coach Certification Programs

The profiles of the training programs are succinct enough to scan, but detailed enough to help you distinguish between programs to decide which may be the best for you.

Coach Spotlights

Coach Spotlights describe the practices of interesting coaches in a variety of specializations to help you see the range of possible tracks for your coaching practice.

Networking Organizations

Described here are the organizations that provide support, ongoing training, referral services, marketing tips, and much more to help you in your coaching practice.

Recommended Resources

Listed here are many books from which you can learn all you want to know and more about coaching.

Interested, but not sure coaching is for you?

Before you invest any money in a training program you might:

- Enlist the services of a life coach yourself. Many coaches offer free or low cost introductory coaching sessions that can help you focus your objectives and goals and determine whether coaching is right for you. If coaching turns out not to be the right thing for you, then she or he can help you discover what will be right for you.
- Check out your local adult education center or community college: Some coaches offer overview classes about how to become a coach, with no obligations or risks. These classes are generally inexpensive ($35–$100). Takeaclass.com is a good place to start—just search on "coaching" in your city.
- Look into some of programs in this book that offer free introductory telecourses (most do). It's also a good way to preview the programs to decide which program is right for you.

ABOUT THE COACH TRAINING PROGRAMS

The information contained in the Profiles in this book was obtained from the Web sites of the individual schools or training programs. Always be sure to refer to the Web site or other contact information listed for the individual school to verify information such as tuition fees and prerequisites.

What should I know about the programs?

If you're not sure what your coach training needs are, talk with a coach or other good listener who can help you determine your preferences and needs. Search for coaches who are doing the kind of work you want to do and find out from them what they did to prepare themselves for the role. ("Coach Spotlights" are a nice place to start.) Contact the prospective school and find out how long they have been in business and what they can tell you about their financial stability. Find out about the qualifications and experience of the school leaders and instructors. Determine what policy the school has for return of tuition or refunds. And finally, find out which other coaching school(s) have a reciprocal arrangement for transferability of courses and activities.

When possible, I have included much of this information in the Profiles. But as with any endeavor, always do your own research to find the best program for you.

Part I: Coach Certification Programs

Abundant Practice: A Program for Coaches

P.O. Box 30523, 4567 Lougheed Hwy,
Suite 201, Burnaby, British Columbia V5C 2J6
Tel: (604) 473-9884, Toll-Free Tel: (800) 610-0970,
Fax: (604) 473-9885, E-mail: teresia@tlcsuccess.com,
Web site: www.tlcsuccess.com

Summary
A series of courses for coaches who want to learn how to build their practice using solid business strategies.

Certification
Program completion meets ICF coach specific training for PCC or MCC designations.

Accreditation
Not accredited

Completion Time
4 months

Course Delivery
Delivered in a series of conference calls, one hour each in length.

Course Locations
Anywhere there is a telephone

Tuition/Fees
The full program is $1295.00.
A payment plan is available.

This series of courses for new, part-time, and experienced coaches is facilitated by Teresia LaRocque, Master Certified Coach. *The Abundant Practice: A Program for Coaches* was co-created with Michael Walsh, a consultant specializing in supporting entrepreneurs. This program has consistent focus on business tools to increase your bottom line. Participants receive support from two experts along with the structure and accountability necessary to build a sustainable practice. It provides a solid business foundation to support new coaches in turning their passion for coaching into a viable business. It focuses on the difference between coaching and the *business* of building a coaching practice, methods to market yourself to clients, and systems for turning potential clients into paying clients.

Program completion meets ICF mentor coach requirements for PCC or MCC designations. The format consists of a one-hour teleclass per week plus unlimited e-mail coaching with Teresia La Rocque and Michael Walsh. To apply to the program, first call Teresia to arrange a telephone interview.

They also offer an additional program, *The Abundant Practice Strategic Support Program*, a program for graduate coaches to help implement the skills they have learned in *The Abundant Practice*. This supplemental program consists of a series of monthly ninety-minute phone calls for $100 per month.

ACADEMY FOR COACH TRAINING

16301 NE 8th Street, Suite 216
Bellevue, WA 98006
Tel: (425) 401-0309
Fax: (425) 401-0311
E-mail: info@coachtraining.com
Web Site: www.coachtraining.com

Summary
Provides comprehensive coaching skills training.

Certification
Provides a Certified Professional Coach designation that exceeds requirements of the International Coach Federation.

Accreditation
Accredited by the International Coach Federation and the NACSAA.

Completion Time
24 weeks

Course Delivery
Four in-person, interactive 2 and 3 day weekend courses and one 24-week integrative teleconference course.

Course Locations
Teleclass available anywhere

Tuition/Fees

The total cost for all courses in the full certification package is $6913.00. Individual courses range from $449.00 to $2895.00.

Fully aligned with the ICF ethics and standards, the *Academy of Coach Training (ACT) Coach Training and Certification Program* provides comprehensive coaching skills training, including interactive in-person instruction, experiential activities, group exercises, and extensive supervised coaching practice. The Academy provides comprehensive training in the core competencies of coaching.

Each of the five modules in the ACT program includes a mix of coaching tools and techniques with "real-time" practice and modeling, with a blend of self-mastery and coaching mastery components. The heart of the curriculum is the Self Mastery/Living Your Vision course. Successful completion of the program, including 130 Student Contact Learning Hours, fulfills a major step towards recognition as a Certified Personal Coach (CPC).

The Living Your Vision® process is the core and foundation of the Academy for Coach Training curriculum. It provides a transformational process of coaching from the inside-out. Students identify their unique vision and purpose, clarify their values, and create a MasterPlan for success, boldly stepping into action. This course includes 12 weeks of one-on-one follow-up coaching with a certified LYV® coach, included in the tuition.

ADD Coaching Academy

17 Googas Road
Slingerlands, NY 12159
Tel: (518) 482-3458
Fax: (518) 482-1221
E-mail: david@addca.com
Web Site: www.addcoachacademy.com

Summary
Provides training for coaches to work with persons with attention deficit disorder.

Certification
ADDCA Coach Graduate (ACG) and Certified ADDCA Coach (COC)

Accreditation
Not accredited

Completion Time
9 months

Course Delivery
All courses are telecourses.

Course Locations
Anywhere there is a telephone

Tuition/Fees
Comprehensive Coaching Program: $3695

ADD Coach Academy offers in-depth training for coaches specializing in working with people who have Attention Deficit Disorder (ADD) and Attention Deficit Hyperactivitiy Disorder (ADHD). ADD clients require coaches with special training and background to understand their special abilities. Coaches learn to support and co-partner with ADD clients to assist in the design of a life plan that accentuates their strengths, skills, and successes.

The curriculum is a nine-month program consisting of once-a-week 90-minute teleclasses, in conjunction with an ADD group coaching lab on alternate months. The focus of the curriculum is to:

- provide the ADD coaching student with an extensive and detailed overview of ADD
- provide the skills necessary to identify clients' strengths, skills, and learning styles
- teach the skills necessary to powerfully coach their clients to achieve consistent progress, and
- provide an understanding of effective positioning and marketing strategies.

Founder and president, David Giwerc, is a Master Certified Coach and former instructor and principal at the Optimal Functioning Institute (see page 72).

COACH SPOTLIGHT:
Vivian M. Rindik, Personal Coach

Vivian M. Rindik is a Coach University-affiliated coach, and a licensed facilitator of the Perfect Life program. Recently featured in *Self* magazine, Vivian is a highly respected member of the worldwide coaching community. Drawing upon over ten years of research in the field of personal development, Vivian's coaching enables her clients to reach unprecedented personal heights.

FAQs with Vivian:

Why hire a coach?

When you know that it is time for a change, it is time to hire a coach. Coaches, professionally trained to focus on the development of human potential, form powerful, insightful relationships to enable their clients to achieve balance in previously frenzied lives, gain an edge in the marketplace, find the perfect mate, maintain profitability, and pursue their life purpose. A combination mentor, taskmaster, motivator and sounding board, a coach will get you on track, keep you focused, and hold you accountable for measurable progress.

What defines a quality coach?

A coach should be a professionally trained individual, committed to their own personal growth and professional conduct. A coach should always honor and support the beliefs, values, individuality, and objectives of their clients. They should become familiar with the personal boundaries of the client, keeping accurate records of all communication, and come to the session focused and prepared. The purpose for the relationship is for the coach to be 100% "there," focusing solely on the well-being and expressed desires of the client.

What is the first step?

All coaches will have their own areas of expertise, and their own style of coaching. Most coaches offer a type of complimentary session, so that the client and coach can get a feel for each other. This is beneficial to both parties, because it is just as important for a coach to evaluate the challenges of the client prior to entering into a relationship.

Web Site: www.personal-coaching.com

Advantage Coaching

324 E. Roosevelt Rd, Suite 206
Wheaton, IL 60187
Tel: (630) 682-8447
Toll-free: (800) 657-5904
Fax: (630) 681-9233
E-mail: info@advantagecoaching.com
Web Site: www.advantagecoaching.com

Summary

Offers two corporate coach training programs through the National Association of Business Coaches.

Certification

Registered Corporate Coach™ (RCC) and Registered Internal Corporate Coach™ (RICC).

Accreditation

Not accredited

Completion Time

About 3 months each.

Course Delivery

RCC program: Either a two-day, in-person seminar or five 90-minute sessions via teleclass. RICC program: Five phases during in-person workshops.

Course Locations
In-person workshops are in Chicago area.
Teleclasses available anywhere.

Tuition/Fees
RCC: $1500 for live class; $1100 for teleclass.

Advantage Coaching and Training offers two coach training programs through the National Association of Business Coaches (NABC). The Registered Corporate Coach™ (RCC) certification is for individuals like coaches, consultants, therapists, mentors, psychologists, and trainers who want to coach executives, managers, and other employees within business environments. The Registered Internal Corporate Coach™ (RICC) certification is designed to train employees of a company, like managers, human resource directors, trainers, supervisors, internal consultants, and other executives to coach other employees within that company.

The RCC and RICC are nationally recognized as specialty certifications for corporate coaches. And, the NABC is the only nationally recognized association for business coaches who work primarily with executives and the only association that offers corporate coach certification for both internal and external coaches. Trainers are professionals who have real world experience working with organizations and Fortune 500 companies.

Extensive details about the RICC and RCC certification prerequisites, requirements, and program goals can be read on www.advantagecoaching.com/certification_programs.asp.

Career Coach Institute

10299 Scripps Trail E-214
San Diego, CA 92131
Toll-free: (866) CCOACH-4
Fax: (208) 692-0574
E-mail: info@careercoachinstitute.com
Web Site: www.careercoachinstitute.com

Summary
A career coach training program resulting in certification

Certification
Offers certification as a Certified Career Coach,™ which is recognized as for credit toward certification through the International Board for Career Management (IBCMC).

Accreditation
Not accredited

Completion Time
6 months

Course Delivery
Via teleclass

Course Locations
Anywhere there is a telephone

Tuition/Fees
Fees range from $1295 (Certified Career Coach)
to $4995 (Master Certified Coach).

The Career Coach Institute offers a six-month virtual training program resulting in certification. Includes required courses in career development, career coach training, and a career coach forum. Class times are based on student needs, and teleconferencing typically includes two 1.5 hour calls and one 1-hour call per week. The Institute also provides a marketing course to help attract clients. Their value-based tuition system allows for taking courses singly or as part of a package that includes additional benefits for business coaches. Special interest courses (at lower fees) are also available for coaches who want to focus on specific topics.

One of the benefits of enrolling in CCI courses is the opportunity to become a Certified Career Coach™. CCI's courses are recognized for credit toward certification through the IBCMC, and can also be used toward certification with the International Coach Federation as a "Portfolio Applicant."

As a Certified Career Coach™, you will have the opportunity to license their course content to instruct your organizational clients and other groups in the CCI systems.

Ciris Alliance: Power Coach Network

208/15 Albert Avenue
Broadbeach, Queensland 4218
Australia
Tel: TBA
Fax:+61-7-5538-8421
E-mail: executive@cirisalliance.com
Web Site: cirisalliance.com/opportunities/trainingprograms.html

Summary

Power Coach training and membership
in the Ciris Alliance

Certification

In-house certification as a Power Coach

Accreditation

Not accredited

Completion Time

3–4 weeks

Course Delivery

Online

Course Locations

Online. In-person practical exercise available in Australia only.

Tuition/Fees
Power Coach Level I: from AUD$500; Level II (Coach): from AUD$500; and Level III (Trainer): from AUD$800

The Ciris Alliance was created in 1999, bringing together an international network of psychologists, graphologists, and management trainers. Its Power Coach Network offers business, personal, and lifestyle coaching services, as well as a Power Coach Training Program. The training is structured into three levels (I, II, and II) and full-time training can take 3–4 weeks to complete. It includes six hours of online coaching with a Power Coach Trainer in their private coaching chat room, unlimited e-mail coaching, and a full day practical exercise with a Power Coach Consultant (available in Australia only). Upon completion of the program, you receive a program diploma and become certified by their Executive Office to practice as a Power Coach.

In this program you will learn:

- the fundamentals of practical psychology
- basic, intermediate, and advanced business coaching techniques
- the fundamentals of good business etiquette and customer service
- effective communication, team-building, and leadership skills
- teaching business body language
- graphology training and more.

COACH SPOTLIGHT:
Diana Haskins, Professional Effectiveness Coach

Diana Haskins has authored *Parent as Coach: Helping Your Teen Build a Life of Confidence, Courage and Compassion.* In this easy-to-read parents handbook, she gives compelling reasons why parents need to adopt a "coaching role" in their relationship with their teens. *Parent as Coach* teaches the seven ways to coach your teen: Respect, Listen, Understand, Appreciate, Support, Promote Responsibility, and Nourish Independence.

As a parent and a certified coach, Diana Haskins has founded and authored *Parent as Coach*. She is a committed parent, successful entrepreneur, author, speaker, trainer and certified Professional Effectiveness Coach (PEC). *Parent as Coach* combines Diana's respect for teenagers with a fresh dynamic perspective on life-coaching.

Diana has received her professional coaching certification from New Ventures West and is active in the International Coaching Federation. Diana is also known for her work as a small business coach, having helped entrepreneurs and service-based professionals build successful businesses all over the U.S.

Diana Haskins coaches and mentors to parents, teenagers, families, and adults who work with teens. She offers individualized coaching to parents, teenagers, and anyone who wants to improve their relationship with young people in a variety of coaching situations, from one-on-one in-person or individual telephone coaching, or in groups in customized family and group coaching, professional presentations and workshops, speaking engagements, and teleclasses.

Recently, Diana has created the Parent as Coach Academy (see page 74) for coaches who want to employ her methods of coaching parents and teens.

Web Site: www.ParentasCoach.com

COACH FOR LIFE

6343 El Cajon Blvd. #138
San Diego, CA 92115
Fax: (619) 287-2577
E-mail: coaching@coachforlife.com
Web Site: www.coachforlife.com

Summary
Courses are based on the Fulfillment Coaching Model.™

Certification
In-house certification programs as Certified Life Coach and Master Certified Life Coach

Accreditation
Master Certified Life Coach Program accredited by the ICF.

Completion Time
CLC: 9 month; MCLC: 9–12 months (additional)

Course Delivery
In-person and teleclasses.

Course Locations
Seminars in various U.S. cities; telecourses available in any location.

Tuition/Fees
CLC program: Parts I and II: $3395
Part III, CLC certification: $3250.
Part IV: $600
Part V, MCLC certification: $3250.
(TOTAL PROGRAM: $10,495)

Coach for Life offers two programs that lead to certification: Certified Life Coach (CLC) Program™ and Master Certified Life Coach (MCLC) Program™. Courses are based on the Fulfillment Coaching Model,™ emphasizing the conscious connection with God/Spirit and an awareness of our innermost qualities and sense of purpose. In this model, the coach's role is to remind the client when he/she has forgotten their innermost connection with Infinite Wisdom/God; to take the client through the self-discovery processes to discover their inner-most values, innate gifts, and life purpose; to be a mirror for clients to reflect back to them their values, aspirations, and life purpose; and to hold an non-judgmental accountability for the things the clients aimed to accomplish.

The Master Certified Life Coach (MCLC) Program is accredited by the International Coach Federation. The MCLC program consists of five parts, the first of which is a five-day in-person seminar. The remaining four parts are delivered via teleclass. [Certified Life Coach (CLC) Program consists of the first three parts of the MCLC program.]

To further the learning experience, the programs offer experiential and meditative exercises, demonstrations and modeling, role playing and interactive group exercises, and an opportunity to coach and be coached.

Coach University (CoachU)

P.O. Box 2124
Salina, KS 67402-2124
Toll Free: (800) 482-6224
Fax: (800) 329-5655
E-mail: info@coachu.com (automated brochure);
help@coachu.com (questions)
Web Site: www.coachu.com

Summary
Provides courses for novice and experienced coach or related professional.

Certification
In-house CoachU Certified Coach Graduate (CCG) and CoachU Certified Master Coach (CCMC) designation

Accreditation
Accredited by the International Coach Federation

Completion Time
2 years

Course Delivery
Telecourses only. Typically provided weekly and consist of 4 one-hour sessions of 20 participants.

Course Locations
Anywhere there is a telephone.

Tuition/Fees
Coach Training Program is $4795.
Payment plans are available.

Created in 1992, CoachU provides courses for novice and experienced coaches or related professionals. CoachU pioneered the delivery of effective training via telecourse. More than 1,000 coaches enter this program every year from all over the U.S., Canada, the United Kingdom, Australia, and at least 25 other countries around the world. CoachU's Coach Training Program (CTP) prepares the coach for certifications offered by CoachU and by the ICF. The program takes about two years to complete and consists of 36 teleclasses and 39 hours of elective courses. Required teleclasses consist of 4 one-hour sessions (one per week).

Requirements for CoachU's in-house certification of Certified Coach Graduate include successful completion of all 36 teleclasses and exams, documentation of the coach's effectiveness with five clients coached, mentoring for at least six months by a Master Certified Coach or Professional Certified Coach, a minimum of 750 hours of coaching experience and at least 40 clients, and a successful interview. For the Certified Master Coach, you must complete a total of 225 hours of coach training, have coached at least 100 clients, for a minimum of 2500 hours.

The Coaches Training Institute (CTI)

1879 Second Street
San Rafael, CA 94901
Tel: (415) 451-6000
Toll Free: (800) 691-6008
Fax: (415) 460-6878
E-mail: info@thecoaches.com
Web Site: www.thecoaches.com

Summary
ICF accredited certification program using the Co-Active Coaching Model.™

Certification
In-house Certified Professional Co-Active Coach designation.

Accreditation
Accredited by the International Coach Federation and NACSAA

Completion Time
6 months

Course Delivery
All courses are teleclasses, except for the final exam, which is done in person.

Course Locations
Anywhere there is a telephone

Tuition/Fees
The Certification Program is $3395. You can take classes a la carte, which totals $4075.

Established in 1992, The Coaches Training Institute (CTI) emphasizes the Co-Active Coaching Model,™ a holistic alliance between client and coach. CTI trains coaches to hold the client as naturally creative, resourceful, and whole; practice the highest standards of professional ethics; be adept at forming partnerships and designing alliances with their clients; establish a thriving coaching practice; hold the client's vision and commitment; and develop their own unique coaching style.

CTI provides courses for the beginning or experienced coach. To become a Certified Professional Co-Active Coach ™ (CPCC), participants take the Co-Active Coaching course and each of four advanced courses: Fulfillment, Balance, Process, and In the Bones. The six-month program consists of weekly group teleconference calls, twelve 2-hour learning labs via telephone, nine 1-hour supervisions, ongoing work with a certified coach, and completion of the certification exam.

If you want to learn more about Co-Active Coaching, CTI sponsors free one-hour bridge line calls so you can get your questions answered directly by CTI Leaders, and hear sample Co-Active Coaching. CTI offers numerous free telecourses and workshops. To learn more, visit their Web site.

COACH SPOTLIGHT:
Tracy Manyfield, Life Coach

Tracy Manyfield is the President and Founder of Partnering a Lifestyle, Inc. Tracy uses her skills, training, and experience in a variety of coaching services, including church coaching, credit report coaching, life coaching, critical coaching skills for managers and executives, professional image coaching, and relationship success training for singles.

As a licensed LifePartnerQuest Relationship Coach, she is qualified to facilitate the Relationship Success Training for Singles. Her certification as a Life Purpose facilitator through Success Unlimited Network allows her to coach people in developing their life purpose statement. In addition, she has completed training in Coaching the Executive through Corporate Coach University International.

Her professional affiliations include the International Coaching Federation, the Christian Life Coaches Network, LifePartnerQuest Coaches Association, and the American Association of Christian Counselors. Tracy is a newly elected Board Member for the Central Ohio Coaches ICF Chapter. She is a study group host for Coachville as well as a Certified Teleclass Leader and Certified PeopleMap Facilitator.

Tracy Manyfield has participated in a wide variety of coach training programs to complement her unique skills and experience. She has trained at: LifePartnerQuest, Success Unlimited Network (SUN), Corporate Coach University International, The Institute for Coach Training, and Coachville.

Tracy has a Bachelor's degree in banking and finance and an Associate's degree in financial technology, as well as twelve years of experience in the finance industry. She has excelled in the areas of leadership, management, strategic planning, customer service, coordinating, teaching, and writing. Her coach training complements her past experience and her unique skills.

Web Site: www.partneringalifestyle.com

COACHING FROM SPIRIT

P.O. Box 836
Saxonburg, PA 16056
Tel: not available
Fax: (413) 832-8228
E-mail: admissions@coachingfromspirit.com
Web Site: www.coachingfromspirit.com

Summary
Training to become a Spirit Coach.

Certification
Leads to status of Certified Master Spirit Coach.

Accreditation
Not accredited

Completion Time
4–12 months

Course Delivery
Teleclass

Course Locations
Anywhere there is a telephone

Tuition/Fees
Living from Spirit (Class 1): $1300
Coaching from Spirit (Class 2): $1300
Certification fees extra.

Coaching from Spirit (CFS) is a coaching process that provides a "divinely guided toolbox of methods, strategies, and approaches to assist in making shifts of consciousness from an ego-centered way of seeing the world to a Spirit (inner) based approach." A Spirit coach works with clients on tangible issues, and offers techniques and tools to bridge the inner and outer worlds in practical ways. Spirit coaching focuses on helping clients make the shifts to more easily create what they desire in life.

CFS Certification Requirements are comprised of three levels. Level One is two 16-week courses, "Living from Spirit," and "Coaching from Spirit." Level Two is a 16-week program of Advanced Coaching. Level Three is the final step to Certified Master Spirit Coach. CFS also offers an optional Level Four for coaching support for coaches seeking an ongoing community and a place to expand your skills.

COACHVILLE

Mailing address not available
Tel: (866) Coachville
E-mail: help@coachville.com
Web Site: www.coachville.com

Summary
Coach training, resources, referral service, and more for low lifetime membership fee.

Certification
In-house Certified Coach designation

Accreditation
Not accredited

Completion Time
Minimum 6 months

Course Delivery
Web-based courses

Course Locations
Anywhere there is Web access.

Tuition/Fees
Lifetime membership is free. Includes complete coach training via the Web.

Coachville claims to be the largest online coach training firm (currently 6,000+members) and provides e-training via interactive, Web-based tools.

Three types of coaches join Coachville:

- Coaches who are already receiving training elsewhere seeking supplemental resources and advanced training
- Coaches who are already coaching successfully for access to new tools and to participate in advanced training
- Individuals who are considering or planning to become a coach

Coachville offers a variety of coach training courses and provides a coach certification that can be obtained in as little as six months, depending on experience. Courses are relevant to beginning as well as experienced coaches and all courses are offered online. Coachville also provides sample coaching sessions in real audio, lists of coaching mistakes, a coach referral network, extensive information on marketing coach services, an in-person conference, and many other support services for coaches.

A life-time membership previously was available for $79, but due to its success, Coachville recently eliminated the membership fee. The reason for the change is their lofty goals: Its founders are aiming to increase the number of coaches in the U.S. from 20,000 to 100,000 by the year 2010, and hopes that free training through Coachville will help attain this goal. Free membership may or may not be a permanent change.

COLLEGE OF EXECUTIVE COACHING

3875 Telegraph Road PMB A115
Ventura, California 93003
Tel: (805) 647-7760
Toll-free: (888) 764-8844
Fax: (805) 647-7660
E-mail: info@executivecoachcollege.com
Web Site: www.executivecoachcollege.com

Summary
Focused on coaching skill and practice development for persons who have obtained or are currently enrolled in advanced degree programs.

Certification
Provides a 72-hour Master Personal and Executive Coach Certification (MPEC)

Accreditation
Some courses are eligible to continuing education credits in some states. See Web site for more information.

Completion Time
72 hours

Course Delivery
Courses offered by in-person workshop basis and by telecourse.

Course Locations
In various cities in California and via teleclass.

Tuition/Fees
In-person courses are typically $165/day and telecourses are typically $565/course.

This program focuses on coaching skills and practice development for people who have obtained or are currently enrolled in advanced degree programs. All courses are taught by persons with doctoral degrees obtained in traditional mental health fields. They offer in-person workshops as well as telecourses.

The Master Personal and Executive Coach (MPEC) Certification Program is accepting applicants and all their courses count toward the 72 hour certification requirements.

Jeffrey E. Auerback, Ph.D., founder and president of the College of Executive Coaching is a licensed psychologist, licensed marriage and family therapist (MFT), personal and executive coach, and an International Coach Federation chapter president. He is the author of *Personal and Executive Coaching: A Guide for Mental Health Professionals*, available at the workshops.

The objectives of the workshops is to understand the differences and similarities between coaching and psychotherapy; to differentiate which clients are suitable for coaching versus psychotherapy; to become familiar with a fundamental coaching protocol and technique; and to become familiar with three principal theorists in coaching. You can download a full-color brochure on the Web site.

COACH SPOTLIGHT:
Susan Martin, Strategy Coach

Susan Martin helps business owners and professionals attract their ideal customers, create extraordinary companies, and make more money doing what they love.

She has 30 years of experience as a entrepreneur. Her clients are from many walks of life: ranging from lawyers, to real estate brokers, to graphic designers, body workers, to writers and clothing designers—anyone who runs a small business or a professional or freelance career, or dreams of doing so.

Many clients who start businesses have a particular professional talent or skill, but don't have the business experience necessary to make it all work. Others may be overwhelmed, or lack focus. Some may want to increase productivity, manage time, or learn how to balance work and personal life. Many come to deal with issues such as marketing, sales, or learning how to manage their finances or maximize their working capital. Some clients need help with setting fees and prices, defining and achieving their goals, or to learn new skills.

Some people come who want to start up a business or change careers; but haven't yet identified what they want to do. Susan helps them to design businesses uniquely suited to their unique personal preferences, interests, talents, skills, experience and lifestyle.

Susan is a working mom. Another important category of clients she works with are moms who work at home, run businesses, or dream of doing so. Many of them want to deal with issues such as avoiding home business scams, balancing work and family, setting boundaries and more. Susan works with clients individually, in groups, and facilitates workshops and seminars.

Susan Martin is a member of the International Coaching Federation (ICF) and the National Association of Business Coaches (NABC).

Web Site: www.thecoachinglounge.com

Comprehensive Coaching U

727 Mallard Place
North Wales, PA 19454
Toll Free: (877) 401-6165
E-mail: contact@coachinginstruction.com
Web Site: www.comprehensivecoachingu.com

Summary
A holistic approach to
coaching skills.

Certification
In-house certification program designated as
Comprehensive Certified Coach

Accreditation
The curriculum is designed to meet the standards established
by the ICF. CCU is not yet accredited, but is applying for ICF accreditation.

Completion Time
12–24 months

Course Delivery
Most courses are conducted via telephone with
supplementary visual material that can be accessed online.

Course Locations
Anywhere there is a telephone.

Tuition/Fees
Certified Comprehensive Coach Program: $3000
Masters Program: $5000
Masters Program without previous
coaching experience: $8000
Fast Tracks Program: $999

Comprehensive Coaching U offers a holistic approach designed by founder Terri Levine. The program builds on natural coaching skills and is open to any professional. CCU offers students the opportunity to choose the coach training program best suited to meet the students' particular needs. Students may further customize their course of study by choosing from a variety of electives and can take as few or as many courses per month as they choose. Only 20 new students are enrolled each month. The curriculum consists of core modules—including lectures and lab classes—and electives that can be selected from 3 tracks. Every CCU coaching skills class has a lab.

The *Certified Comprehensive Coaching Skills Program* (CCCS) is for individuals seeking advanced coaching skills, as well as to fulfill ICF's Professional Coach Certification (PCC) and Master Coach Certification (MCC) requirement of at least 125 hours of coaching specific training. The CCCS consists of 34 classes and students may customize their training by choosing either the *Practice Building Track* or the *Organizational Coaching Track*.

Corporate Coach University International

P.O. Box 2800-331
Carefree, AZ 85377
Tel: (800) 482-6224; (719) 266-8057
Fax: (800) 329-5655; (508) 533-9012
E-mail: admissions@coachinc.com
Web Site: www.ccui.com

Summary

Certification program in business coaching for managers and professionals.

Certification

In-house certification as Certified Corporate Business Coach and Advanced Certified Corporate Business Coach

Completion Time

6–12 weeks

Accreditation

Not accredited

Course Delivery

All courses for the Business Coach program are telecourses.

Course Locations

Business coach telecourses can take place anywhere.

Tuition/Fees

The full teleclass curriculum leading to Business Coach Certification is $3595.
Coach U students receive a discount (see Web site).
Advanced: $3000 for panel interview administration

Corporate Coach U International offers a Business Coaching Certification Program. The program provides a methodology for managers, coaches, and others to create a collaborative, growth-enhancing environment at any given time in any given situation. The program is for internal and external coaches, managers, trainers, consultants, and other professionals desiring personal development in interpersonal communications through coaching.

The program includes fifteen modules, covering basic through advanced corporate and business coaching skills. Classes are six weeks, eight weeks, or twelve weeks, depending on the module, with weekly class sessions of 90 minutes or 60 minutes.

The Corporate Coaching Program (CBCP) has two levels of certification: Certified Corporate Business Coach (Basic Level) and Advanced Certified Corporate Business Coach. The advanced certified corporate business coach designation is aligned with the ICF's requirements for Professional Certified Coach.

The Advanced designation is obtained with the basic certification, plus a series of observed coaching sessions, letters of recommendation, and a panel interview, which costs extra (see above).

EDUCOACH—THE EDUCATION COACH TRAINING COMPANY

16697 North 108th Way
Scottsdale, AZ 85259
Tel: (480) 515-5220
E-mail: director@educoach.com
Web Site: www.educoach.com

Summary
Coach training using the Totally Coached School™ Model.

Certification
No

Accreditation
Not accredited

Completion Time
12 weeks

Course Delivery
Teleclasses have a maximum enrollment of 20 per class and are scheduled for one hour per week, four times per month.

Course Locations
Anywhere a telephone is available

Tuition/Fees
$1500

EduCoach® uses the Totally Coached School™ Model, which brings out the promise in each individual. Specializes in working with educators, students, and teachers. Some courses focus on coaching teens and children; professional development credit available. Three programs are available, including Coaching for Life, Superintendent to Superintendent, and Executive to Executive, as well as custom coach training.

The EduCoach® Method is a blend of coaching and technology. The method includes continuous, ongoing support of coaching and a job-embedded learning environment, made possible through teleconferencing. Coaching can be customized.

These programs are not meant for the individual who intends to become a "personal coach" in private practice. Rather, EduCoach® seeks to teach coaching to people who want to bring it to their established areas of expertise or their organization.

COACH SPOTLIGHT:
Heather Richardson Cameron, Educational Coach

Coaching for the College (and College-Bound) Student

Heather Richardson Cameron is a lifelong learner and educator. She provides coaching for college and college-bound students.

What is Educational Coaching?

"Attending college can be one of the most rewarding experiences in your life. The knowledge gained, friends made, and skills learned provide a basic platform on which the rest of your life can be built.

Attending college can also be one of the most stressful, time-consuming, and financially impacting experiences in your life. Driving a 20-year-old car, working the night shift, social life made up entirely of study groups—these are the sacrifice made by students who are pursuing that strong platform.

It makes sense, therefore, to get the most gain for the least pain from your college experiences. That is where educational coaching comes in. There are many factors that contribute to a successful educational experience, which we have divided into the 8 categories: 1) What to study; 2) Where to study; 3) Getting in; 4) Paying for it; 5) Studying; 6) Fun; 7) Problems; 8) Graduating—what now?"

Heather's clients include students who are attending a local community college, moving to an Ivy League university across the country, taking an online business course, first time students, returning students, first generation college students, and parents.

Heather has a B.A. in Liberal Studies from Humboldt State University (Arcata, CA) and an M.A. in Education and Human Development from The George Washington University (Washington, D.C.). She is also a member of the ICF and a founding member of Coachville (see page 34).

Her professional affiliations include the American Association for Higher Education, the American Association of University Women, the Association for the Study of Higher Education, and the National Association for Women in Education.

Web Site: www.learninginnovations.net

Executive Coach Academy

201 West 74th Street, Suite #14F
New York, NY 10023
Tel: (212) 501-7666
Fax: (212) 873-6809
E-mail: programquestions@executivecoachacademy.com
Web Site: www.executivecoachacademy.com

Summary
Sixteen week executive coaching program.

Certification
Does not provide certification

Accreditation
Not accredited

Completion Time
16 weeks

Course Delivery
Basic program is via telecourse.
Elective two-day weekend
course is in-person.

Course Locations
Weekend course is usually held in New York.
Telecourse available anywhere.

Tuition/Fees
Program is $1950 in advance or
$2100 if made in installments.

The Executive Coach Academy Program is a sixteen week, two hours per week distance learning program. They also offer weekend seminars as an optional part of the training program. As part of the program, coaching candidates can elect to attend a two-day weekend (usually in New York City) or instead choose to receive six individual 45-minute coaching sessions by an ECA-approved coach.

The program's lessons include:
- how to engage a client on the telephone
- how a coaching conversation is different than a regular conversation with a friend
- how to run telephone groups
- the nuts and bolts of how to build a coaching practice
- how to use e-mail effectively
- how to establish a niche as a coach and how this can make a difference in your practice, and more.

Program director Jeremy Robinson is a Master Certified Coach (ICF certified) and has been doing coaching and consulting for more than 15 years. He serves on the Corporate Coach Committee at the ICF and runs a monthly telephone conference call devoted to Best Practices in Corporate Coaching.

Fill Your Coaching Practice

Mailing address unavailable.
Web Site: www.fillyourpractice.com

Summary
Offers an 8-week condensed training program.

Certification
Does not offer certification

Accreditation
Not accredited

Completion Time
8 weeks

Course Delivery
Combination of recorded teleclasses,
online handouts, and hands-on assignments

Course Locations
Anywhere

Tuition/Fees
$97 to download the program online

Fill Your Practice offers a number of coaching classes, including an 8-week training program to help coaches obtain clients. It's a combination of weekly online recorded teleclasses, live group coaching, one-on-one mentoring, e-mail support, class notes, online handouts, and hands-on assignments.

The weekly lessons that teach the secrets of attracting quality new clients include:

- How to Win Your Ideal Clients with Speed and Comfort
- How to Develop Your Own Desirable and Trusted Brand
- How to Project a Positive Image that Precedes You
- How to Instantly Build Rapport with Prospects and Clients
- How to Reach a Wide Audience with the Perfect Message
- How to Present Yourself Professionally with Warmth and Style
- How to Build a Sustaining Practice using Digital Technology
- How to Become a Center of Influence and Capture Media Attention

International Coach Academy

P.O. Box 307272
Columbus, OH 43230-9998
Toll-free: (866) 476-9655
Fax: (614) 475-2853
E-mail: info@icoachacademy.com
Web Site: www.icoachacademy.com

Summary
Coach training for both the beginner
and practicing coach

Certification
In-house certification

Accreditation
Not accredited, but the programs are aligned
with ICF training requirements.

Completion Time
Programs are available at
your own pace for 6 to 24 months.

Course Delivery
Teleclass and online

Course Locations
Anywhere there is a telephone

Tuition/Fees
Professional Certified Coach Program (PCCP): $3800
Associate Certified Coach Program (ACCP): $2624

Formerly Coach Campus, The International Coach Academy offers coach training via a combination of teleclasses, lecture notes inside a virtual classroom, and tutorials. They offer two certification programs: Professional Certified Coach Program and Associate Certified Coach Program. They are designed for people who want to become a part-time or full-time professional coach, or for people wanting to develop their coaching skills. You can focus on personal coaching, business coaching, or both.

Associate Certified Coach is particularly suitable for managers, consultants, therapists, financial planners, and personal trainers who want to develop an additional service for their clients or incorporate coaching skills into their existing business.

Both programs provide an International Coach Academy certification. The training has been designed around, and is aligned with the competencies of the International Coach Federation. Students receive certification and upon graduation will have the necessary hours to achieve the Professional Coach Certification of the ICF (International Coaching Federation).

COACH SPOTLIGHT:
Christopher Ashe, Whole Life Personal Coach

The Joy of Helping People

"Ever since I can remember one of my great joys has been to help people to be all that they can be. In college I majored in sociology because of my curiosity about how society functions. As a medic in Viet Nam and later working as an emergency room and operating room technician I had the privilege of helping people during some of their greatest periods of stress. For most of my working life I have been involved in management and training for entrepreneurial and start-up companies in entertainment and performing arts, recreation, and real estate. I loved this work because I have been able to help individuals and businesses turn their dreams into reality.

I have also been a teacher and trainer of adults and was recognized as *Educator of the Year by the Connecticut Association of Realtors*®. Now as a coach I can do even more to help people grow their dreams. Why? Because as an outsider without a vested interest in the outcome I can ask the tough questions that the insider never dares to ask. Whether I am coaching an individual or a group, I can put my whole being into moving them where they want to go, not where I think they should go."

Christopher's Coaching Philosophy:

Every person has within them the core ingredients necessary for achieving all the success, prosperity and happiness they seek. The role of the coach is to help the individual to define the specific goals, discover the internal core ingredients, develop the framework for success, acquire the information and skills needed for the task and provide unlimited rational encouragement throughout the process.

Christopher is a LifePartnerQuest Relationship Coach for Singles and Coachville-affiliated coach.

Web Site: www.coachunlimited.com

Institute for Life Coach Training (formerly Therapist University)

2801 Wakonda Drive
Ft. Collins, Colorado 80521
Tel: 888-267-1206
Fax: 970-224-9832
E-mail: info@lifecoachtraining.com
Web Site: www.lifecoachtraining.com

Summary

A program for therapists, counselors, human services professionals, and others who want to learn coaching skills.

Certification

In-house certification as Certified Life Coach. The curriculum can count towards the hours necessary to achieve the ICF's Professional Coach Certification.

Accreditation

Not accredited

Completion Time

15 weeks-6 months

Course Delivery

All courses are teleclasses.

Course Locations
Anywhere there is a telephone

Tuition/Fees
Tuition for the basic 30-hour course is $1695 and includes all course materials.

This program is designed primarily by therapists for human service professionals who want to learn and develop coaching skills. It focuses on teaching coaching skills (as well as business and marketing tools) without any repetition of skills already developed. It also offers a number of advanced courses for experienced coaches. Advanced courses are provided in relationship coaching, corporate coaching, family business coaching, group coaching, assessment as part of coaching, and advanced marketing.

All classes are taught by teleconference calls with 10 to 25 other students. Instructors are all former therapists who have built successful coaching practices. Classes are one hour, twice a week for 15 weeks. In addition, students receive free once-a-month alumni calls, free frequent Q&A calls, and a Coach Referral Service.

The Certified Life Coach designation consists of 30 hours of basic training, 40 additional hours of supervised reading and peer coaching hours, 6 months of being coached, and submitting 6 tapes of client coaching sessions to be reviewed for coaching skills competency.

Kadmon Academy of Human Potential

Box BCM-3695
London WC1N 3XX
United Kingdom
Tel: (020) 7919 6032
Fax: (020) 7919 6032
E-mail: lifecoaching@ukprofessionals.com
Web Site: www.lifecoaching.ukprofessionals.com

Summary
Coach training program with a holistic approach to coaching.

Certification
Provides a Diploma in Life Coaching plus post-qualification specialist study leading to Certification as a Life and Personal Coach.

Accreditation
Accredited by the Counseling and Psychotherapy Society (UK)

Completion Time
12 months+

Course Delivery
Textbooks, course manuals, written assignments, written practicum/activity reports, and e-mail tutor support and coaching.

Course Locations
Worldwide (distance learning)

Tuition/Fees

Diploma in Life Coaching: GBP 995.00 (approx. US$1500.00);
Diploma in Life Coaching (Distinction): GBP 1250.00
Certified Personal and Life Coach Certification: GBP 495.00

The Kadmon Academy of Human Potential was founded by hypnotherapist and psychotherapist Morris Berg, Ph.D. The Kadmon Academy offers courses in a range of holistic fields, which have been created by Kadmon's own tutors and by a network of linked training providers. Kadmon provides a distance learning course in holistic life coaching, including counseling skills, stress reduction, and metaphor work. Their perspective is integrative, drawing from different coaching models.

Graduates receive a Diploma in Life Coaching (DLC) and can proceed to extra certification as a Certified Personal and Life Coach (CPLC). The Diploma course is now accredited by the Counseling and Psychotherapy Society (UK) and leads to Licentiate membership of the Society. Student membership of the Society is given to all students for one year, included in the course fee.

The program focuses a traditional distance learning using printed materials rather than audio tapes or digital recordings delivered over the Internet. As well as standard coaching methods, specific topics and techniques featured include stress reduction, relaxation, breathing, brief meditation, and more. Assignments are generally exchanged and reviewed via mail or e-mail.

The only entry qualification for the program is a good standard general education (formally certified or self-taught) and a good level of written/spoken English.

Life on Purpose Institute

1160 W. Blue Ridge Road
P.O. Box 834
Flat Rock, NC 28731
Tel: (828) 697-9239
Fax: (828) 697-6038
E-mail: brad@lifeonpurpose.com
Web Site: www.lifeonpurpose.com/coachtrain.html

Summary
Training and certification as a Life on Purpose Coach.

Certification
In-house certification as Life on Purpose Certified Coach.

Accreditation
Not accredited

Completion Time
Approximately 12 months

Course Delivery
Teleclass

Course Locations
Anywhere there is a telephone

Tuition/Fees

Tuition plans vary by the method of payment.
Full payment: $2950.

Training and certification as a Life on Purpose Coach using The Purpose Process,™ a systematic process for clarifying your life purpose and living true to it. Offers three coaching categories: Life Purpose Coach, Life on Purpose Certified Coach, and Life on Purpose Faculty Coach.

Coaching students begin by going through The Purpose Process™ themselves. Next, they further develop coaching skills by pairing up with other coach interns and by coaching your first clients. Virtual classroom work is supplemented by group coaching sessions. The program also provides training in practice building and abundance training.

As a supplement to your learning, they also provide you with access to their Purpose Process Online Program (PPOP). This web based program combines an interactive module-by-module tutorial with Real Audio recording of an actual group coaching class on the first stage of the Purpose Process.

COACH SPOTLIGHT:
Deborah Brown, Career Coach

Deborah Brown is a career and mentor coach who has worked with executives, professional, entrepreneurs, and coaches helping them to witness results in their careers and in their lives since August 1998. She focuses on her clients transitioning into careers they love, advancing in the careers they have now, while still finding time for themselves. She believes anything is possible once your have a plan to get there.

Before becoming a coach, Deborah spent 12 years in sales and marketing for Fortune 500 companies and dot-coms. She has a B.A. in Marketing from Hofstra University and a Certificate in Financial Planning from New York University.

Q&A with Deborah Brown

Who works with a Career Coach?

Someone who is tired of being in a career that makes them unhappy. Someone who wants more and is ready to make it happen for themselves.

What do you focus on with your clients?

I focus on empowering them, so they can create a career and a life they love. We discuss how they can overcome obstacles, fears, and limiting beliefs. They learn how to believe in themselves, recognize their accomplishments, and trust their judgment.

How does a client get started?

You can set up a 30-minute Get Acquainted and Goal Setting telephone call to see if career coaching is the next step for you. You can also check out my Web site's self-test, "How Coachable Are You?" (www.surpassyourdreams.com/test.html) to see if you're ready for coaching.

Deborah is a graduate of Coach University's Coaches Training Program and President of CoachU's Long Island-Nassau County chapter. She is a member of the ICF, the National Career Development Association, and the Association for Job Search Trainers.

Deborah is a published motivational writer whose articles can be found on more than 50 Web sites. She is the resident Career Coach for PowerHomeBiz.com and has published an e-book entitled *Living a Life You Love: The Pathway to Personal Freedom.*

Web Site: www.surpassyourdreams.com

Life Purpose Institute

8775 Aero Drive Suite 233
San Diego, CA 92123-1779
Tel: (858) 573-0888
Fax: (858) 573-0899
E-mail: information@lifepurposeinstitute.com
Web Site: www.lifepurposeinstitute.com

Summary
Coach training program in life purpose and career coaching using the Life Purpose Process©.

Certification
In-house certification as Certified Life Purpose Coach.

Accreditation
Not accredited

Completion Time
In-person: 4 days
Teleclass: 13 weeks

Course Delivery
Four-day in-person workshop or 13-week teleclass.

Course Locations
In-person workshop takes place in San Diego, CA. Teleclass available worldwide.

Tuition/Fees
Four-day intensive: $1895
13-week teleclass: $2295

The Life Purpose Institute trains coaches in the Life Purpose Process©, a method for helping people discover their life purpose and find the work they love. It is an experiential, results-oriented process that recognizes and honors each person's uniqueness and needs.

The Institute offers two options for training: a four-day intensive workshop held in San Diego, CA and a 13-week telephone course. The four-day workshop is held twice a year and is limited to 12 people. The 13-week telephone course starts over regularly—check the Web site for the next start date. The telephone course takes place once a week for 2 hours for 13 consecutive weeks. The training combines teleconferencing calls, written exercises, and practice sessions for you to complete on your own. Participating in the 13 week period allows you time to absorb the material from their 450 page manual, practice the exercises, and receive coaching for the full training program. Certification is granted when you are able to demonstrate your ability to provide life purpose and career coaching/consulting.

To participate in this program you need at least a bachelor's degree and some life experience working with people.

Live Your Dream by Joyce Chapman

PMB #111
826 Orange Ave
Coronado, CA 92118-2698
Tel: (541)994-9971
Fax (541)994-9967
Web Site: www.joycechapman.com

Summary
Dream and journaling coaching based on
Joyce Chapman's bestselling books.

Certification
In-house certification
as Dream Coach or Journaling Coach.

Accreditation
Not accredited

Completion Time
3–6 months+

Course Delivery
A combination of at-home assignments, 30-minute coaching phone consultations, and written feedback and recommendations.

Course Locations
Worldwide

Tuition/Fees
Fee options vary. Basic program with coaching: $1,000–$1,500.

Joyce Chapman provides personal and professional coaching, training, and certification programs, based her bestselling books, *Live Your Dream* and *Journaling for Joy*.

Live Your Dream is a step-by-step program to discover and achieve your life purpose by listening to your inner wisdom and being true to who you are as well as who you would like be become. *Journaling for Joy* is about writing your way to personal growth and freedom using special journaling techniques.

In the Home Study program, students participate in workbook assignments which are read and critiqued by Joyce Chapman. Upon completion of the program, the client may choose to go on to the Certification Program enabling them to coach or facilitate others in the chosen program. Students may choose from six options of the Home Study program, integrating critiqued workbook assignments, phone sessions, additional feedback, independent workbook work, and coaching/consultations with Joyce. See Web site for more detail.

Students receive a coaching manual, eight 30-minute coaching phone consultations, written feedback and recommendations, a right to use all copyrighted *Live Your Dream* books, workbooks, and materials, and a Certificate of Training upon completion.

MentorCoach

4400 East West Highway #1104
Bethesda, MD 20814
Tel: (301) 986-5688
Fax: (301) 913-9447
E-mail: info@mentorcoach.com
Web Site: www.mentorcoach.com

Summary
Provides working, licensed therapists with knowledge and skills to add coaching to their practice.

Certification
In-house MentorCoach Training Program (MCP). MentorCoach Certification Track in development.

Accreditation
Not accredited

Completion Time
6 months

Course Delivery
Basic training consists of 24 one-hour teleclasses.

Course Locations
Anywhere there is a telephone

Tuition/Fees
MentorCoach Training Program: $1995

MentorCoach was created in 1998 to provide working, licensed therapists with the knowledge and skills to add coaching practice to their ongoing clinical work. It provides participants with free teleconference bridges and entire virtual groups to lead. It is particularly suitable to doctoral level therapists. MentorCoach doesn't teach basic skills and values, because therapists have already mastered those skills.

The program takes place via tele-conferencing and e-mail over a period of six months. MentorCoach is approved by the American Psychological Association, the National Association of Social Workers, the National Board of Certified Counselors, and the California Board of Behavioral Sciences to offer continuing education for psychologists, social workers, certified counselors, and California-based Marriage Family Therapists.

The basis of the program is the MentorCoach Training Program (MCP), which consists of 24 one-hour teleclasses (once a week for six months). MentorCoach is in the process of creating a MentorCoach Certification Track Program for those who value and desire professional certification. The certification program will include the basic training as well as additional training, coaching experience, and a final exam.

COACH SPOTLIGHT:
Barbara Garro, M.A., Weight Loss and Weight Management Coach

Weight Loss and Weight Management Coaching

Barbara Garro, M.A. provides weight loss and weight management coaching. She focuses on nine life-enhancing results of coaching:

- move from problem-thinking toward solution-thinking
- move from chance toward intentional choice
- move from unrewarding activities toward joyfully living your dreams
- move from relationship puzzles toward understanding
- move from suffocating under other's control toward personal freedom
- move from the hurt of other's criticism toward the pride of positive identity
- move from bad habits that hold you back toward good habits that move you forward
- move from pitiful starvation of struggle to a passionate banquet of self-achievement
- move from the weakness of self-doubt to the strength of self-confidence

Barbara invites clients to begin a journey to discover what you eat, why you eat, when you eat, and what bad eating habits have formed. She aims to create a positive conversation between you and your body. She believes that learning to listen to your body is half the weight loss battle.

Barbara Garro, M.A., is a professional coach, speaker, and author or *Grow Yourself a Life You'll Love.*

Garro maintains professional memberships in The Institute of Noetic Sciences, Association for Psychological Type, International Enneagram Association, International Women's Writing Guild, Academy of American Poets, and the Association for Transpersonal Psychology.

Web Site: www.electricenvisions.com

OPTIMAL FUNCTIONING INSTITUTE

903 Luttrell Street, Suite 1
Knoxville, TN 37917
Tel: (423) 524-9549
Fax: (423) 637-8831
Web Site: www.addcoach.com

Summary

A comprehensive ADD coach training program.

Certification

Not currently available

Accreditation

Not accredited

Completion Time

15–18 months

Course Delivery

Telephone courses supplemented with a mentoring system, manuals, and workbooks

Course Locations

Anywhere with telephone connection

Tuition/Fees

The price for the comprehensive program is $3250 plus long distance telephone charges.

The Optimal Functioning Institute was established in 1994 to train coaches to identify, understand, and coach clients with Attention Deficit Disorder (ADD). The training is meant to benefit mental health professionals, ADD professionals, non-ADD coaches, human resource professionals, parents, and high-functioning ADDers, among others. The training teaches how to identify, understand, and coach a person with ADD; understand the makeup of the ADD brain; become aware of the most current information about ADD and ADD coaching; and to experience coaching clients with ADD while you train.

The program includes 15 monthly modules (1 hour per week for 4 weeks), weekly homework assignments, monthly coaching labs, and exam-review sessions. Students are expected to also read additional required books about ADD.

Graduation requirements include:

- 68 hours TeleClass training
- 36 hours peer coaching (1/2-hr/wk; 18 months)
- 40 hours ADD coaching (paid)
- 50 hours Coaching Labs (several 2-hour labs available monthly)
- 5 hours Clinic supervision for Clinic Coaches
- Passing the graduation exam.

Parent as Coach Academy

P.O. Box 14032
Portland, OR 97293
Tel: (503) 236-6103
Fax: (240) 526-0852
E-mail: info@parentascoach.com
Web Site: www.parentascoach.com

Summary
Coaching training for working with parents, teens, and families

Certification
Not available

Accreditation
Not accredited

Completion Time
6 months

Course Delivery
Teleclasses and 2 in-person workshops.

Course Locations
Via telephone and in Portland, OR

Tuition/Fees
Program fee: $2700
$3500 for European-based training

Parent as Coach Academy offers a rigorous six-month training for service professionals and lay persons who are coaches, teachers, clergy, trainers, therapists, counselors, mentors, community leaders, youth workers or active parents who want to lead and teach others. It is grounded in a TRIAD approach, with three basic learning modes:

- a strong coaching foundation,
- coaching teens, parents and families,
- business/practice building—bringing coaching into the world.

The goal of the Academy is to teach a coaching skill set that can be utilized in the community in a variety of settings: coaching, workshops, classes, public speaking and other applications. Each participant is expected to participate fully and powerfully in growing their own capacities, supporting the other students, and staking their claim in the world in the advocacy for young people, parents and families.

Requirements for Admission to Program include: existing status/role as a professional coach, therapist, councilor, teacher, or clergy (some exceptions made); a letter of intent; and an interview with Diana Haskins (read more about Diana on page 23).

Relationship Coaching Institute

P.O. Box 111783
Campbell, CA 95011
Tel: (408) 261-3332
Web Site: www.relationshipcoachinginstitute.com

Summary
Relationship coach training and membership support

Certification
Provides two levels of in-house certification for working with singles and two levels of certification for working with couples

Accreditation
Not accredited

Completion Time
Varies by class

Course Delivery
All courses offered by teleclass

Course Locations
Worldwide

Tuition/Fees
One-time enrollment fee of $495.
Monthly membership dues:

$29/month for Singles Coaching Training
and $49 for Singles/Couples Coaching Training.

The Relationship Coaching Institute (RCI) provides relationship coaching training and support for helping professionals. Services are dedicated to helping singles and couples have successful life partnerships. They define relationship coaching as a professional client-focused service that assumes that individuals are healthy, powerful, and able to achieve their relationship goals with effective support, information, and guidance.

RCI offers two training programs: *Singles Coaching Training and Licensing Program* and *Singles and Couples Coaching Training and Licensing Program*.

RCI's relationship coaching training includes lifetime membership in their coaching community with numerous benefits. The one-time enrollment fee is $495 with monthly dues of $29 for Singles Coaching Training, or $49 for Singles/Couples Coaching Training. RCI member benefits include all trainings, license for use of RCI materials, ongoing teleclass trainings and conference calls, mentoring and technical support, your own RCI Web site, RCI community listserv for networking, ideas, and support, Practice Building Program, and marketing support.

RCI also offers a number of free recorded teleclasses, including Introduction to Relationship Coaching for Singles and Pre-commitment Coaching for New Couples. For the client-oriented side of this company, visit www.lifepartnerquest.com.

COACH SPOTLIGHT:
Dr. Harriet Kramer Becker and Dr. John Becker, Relationship Coaches

SinglestoSoulmates™

Dr. Harriet Kramer Becker and Dr. John Becker help people learn about the skills and nuances of attracting and deepening a Romantic Soulmate Relationship, as well as about giving the love that heals to children, friends, and others. Both Harriet and John are professional therapists with extensive experience in working with singles and couples and families.

Services for Single Adults include:
- Conscious Dating: Relationship Success Program for Singles Relationship Success Training for Singles
- Advanced Singles Coaching Team
- Private Singles Coaching and Therapy
- Imago Relationship Insight Group
- Imago Relationship Group Therapy

Services for Couples include:
- Imago Relationship Insight Group
- Imago Relationship Group Therapy
- Partners in Life—a program for pre-commitment couples
- Private Imago Relationship Coaching and Therapy

The Psychotherapy and Coaching Practices of Harriet Kramer Becker, Ph.D. and John Becker, Ph.D., LLC, has offices in metro Washington, D.C., Miami Beach, and Fort Lauderdale, FL.

Dr. Harriet Kramer Becker and Dr. John Becker ore Certified Imago Therapists and Certified LifePartnerQuest Coaches with specialized training in helping singles and couples, as well as families.

Web Site: www.singlestosoulmates.com

Results Life Coaching

U.S. Operations:
47 Clive Street
Metuchen, NJ 08840-1060
Tel: (866) 854-5433
Fax: (732) 494-4495
E-mail: rlcnj@resultslifecoaching.com
Web Site: www.resultslifecoaching.com

Summary
A life coaching training program

Certification
Provides in-house certification program

Accreditation
Not accredited, but courses count toward coach specific training by the ICF.

Completion Time
12 weeks

Course Delivery
Distance learning program via telephone and Internet.

Course Locations
Via teleconference calls and the Internet. Also has a face-to-face program in various locations in the U.S. and Australia.

Tuition/Fees
Intensive Coach Training Program: US$2995

Results Life Coaching (RLC) provide a comprehensive training curriculum consisting of 24 modules of intensive coach training, a wide range of continuing education, and specializations in personal, business, or executive coaching. You train from anywhere in the world via distance learning. RLC has offices all over the world, although their global headquarters is in Australia.

The Intensive Coach Training Program is can be taken face-to-face in various locations in the U.S., Australia, and New Zealand, or via distance learning. The distance learning program is built around 24 one-hour teleconference calls run twice a week, plus homework, self study, and e-mail work. During the training you will learn about: the qualities of a great coach, powerful communication, the dance of coaching, how to create real change, how to build trust and intimacy, how to uncover a core issue, developing goals, designing actions, and building a coaching practice.

Additional opportunities with RLC include becoming a mentor to other coaches, becoming a professional trainer leading their programs, becoming a regional host (someone responsible for developing a local community of coaches in their region), and becoming a franchise owner (their first overseas franchise is currently running in New Jersey, U.S.).

# Part II: Networking Organizations

American Coaching Association, www.quicksitemaker.com/members/americoach/

The American Coaching Association provides training and membership benefits to people seeking to become ADD coaches, practicing coaches who want to deepen their skills, and health care professionals who want to enhance their effectiveness with ADDers.

Christian Coaches Network (CCN), www.christiancoaching.com

A diverse group of trained coaches representing various denominations, coaching specialties, and life experience. Their Web site provides a find-a-Christian coach service and a description of their Certified Christian Coach designation.

Coachville, www.coachville.com

Coachville is the largest network of coaches with a continuous focus on assisting coaches to improve their skills and develop their practices. See their coach training page (page 34) for an in-depth description.

International Association of Personal and Professional Coaches (IAPBC), www.extremeachievers.com/coaches

IAPBC is an independent body for personal and business coaching certification, setting a standard for coaching services worldwide and promoting the profession for the benefit of members and their clients.

It is dedicated to advancing the art and value of experts who coach individuals and companies by setting and implementing standards for certification; promoting the profession and the importance of selecting a certified coach; providing opportunities for professional development; fostering community; and developing strategic partnerships.

International Coach Federation (ICF), www.coachfederation.org

The ICF is the primary professional association for coaches. They provide an extensive number of benefits and services, including two levels of certification (Master Certified Coach and Professional Certified Coach), coaching school accreditation, conferences, standards and ethical guidelines, a coach referral service, and much more.

International Consortia of Business Coaches (I-CBC), www.i-cbc.com

This group was formed to create a global network of business coaches to generate opportunities for collaboration and teaming. There are four membership levels: professional, member, affiliate, and student. They also provide a certification program as a Certified Business Coach.

International Federation of Professional Coaches and Mentors (IFPCM), www.ifpcm.org

The IFPCM exists to build, support, and preserve the integrity of the coaching profession. They hold regular workshops, conferences, and conventions to support this mission.

International Mentoring Association, www.wmich.edu/conferences/mentoring/

The International Mentoring Association, housed at Western Michigan University, was established in 1988 in response to the growing need for an organized forum focusing on innovative mentoring ideas and practices. The Association, now a worldwide organization, unites a broad cross-section of individuals interested in the theory and practice of effective mentoring. Every member brings a diverse and unique perspective from the various fields of mentoring that each represents.

National Association of Business Coaches (NABC), www.mynabc.org

The NABC is a business-to-business coaching organization designed primarily for business coaches who work with small business owners, executives, managers, supervisors, and directors in organizations across North America.

North American Coaching School Accreditation Agency (NACSAA), 199-2805 East Oakland Park Blvd, Fort Lauderdale, FL 33306-1813

The NACAAA reviews coaching schools and programs throughout the world to determine their suitability, validity, foundation, and value. The agency gathers data from several sources, including printed materials distributed by the individual schools and programs and information available on the Internet. NACSAA uses the information from these sources to assess each individual school. To receive accredited status, a school must achieve a point total minimum of 90 points.

Professional Coach and Mentors Association (PCMA), www.pcmaonline.com

This organization provides networking and referral services and professional development opportunities for its members. PCMA serves professional coaches and mentors, and successful professionals expanding into these areas, by offering quality programs for developing professional skills and building successful practices, while connecting professional coaches/mentors with each other and the users of their services.

Part III: Recommended Resources

This list was compiled from the Web sites of various coaches who recommended these books for beginner and practicing coaches. All are available at bn.com, borders.com, and amazon.com.

Callings: Finding and Following an Authentic Life
by Gregg Michael Levoy

How do we know if we're following our true callings? How do we sharpen our senses to cut through the distractions of everyday reality and hear the calls that are beckoning us? *Callings* is the first book to examine the many kinds of calls we receive and the great variety of channels through which they come to us. A calling may be to do something (change careers, go back to school, have a child) or to be something (more creative, less judgmental, more loving). Drawing on the hard-won wisdom and powerful stories of people who have followed their own calls, Gregg Levoy shows us the many ways to translate a calling into action.

Co-Active Coaching: New Skills for Coaching People Toward Success in Work and Life
by Laura Whitworth, Henry House, Phil Sandahl, Henry Kimsey-House

Whether you're training coaches, instituting a mentoring program, or evaluating a coach for your own use, the authors' model will come in handy. This book proposes a kind of coaching that involves the active participation of both the coach and the client. Written by the founders of The Coaches Training Institute (CTI) (see page 28), this book is a must-read for those considering a coaching career and for those who want to know more about how a using personal coach can enhance their lives.

Coaching for Performance: People Skills for Professionals
by John Whitmore

John Whitmore has written a book for the service industry of the 90s: personal and professional coaching. It can help you learn the skills and the art of good coaching, and realize its value in unlocking people's potential to maximize their own performance. The book contains extensive examples of effective questions for generating awareness and responsibility that compel the client to think, demand high-resolution focus, and provide the coach with a feedback loop. Sections on motivation and building self-esteem through coaching are included.

Masterful Coaching: Extraordinary Results by Impacting People and the Way They Think and Work Together
by Robert Hargrove

Written as an interactive dialogue with the reader, *Masterful Coaching* emphasizes core coaching skills—sponsoring, counseling, acknowledging, teaching, and confronting. Hargrove shows you how to unearth what people passionately care about, reach breakthrough goals, and implement transformational change. It provides you with the ideas, methods, and tools to make the difference you have always wanted to make.

The Portable Coach: 28 Surefire Strategies for Business and Personal Success
by Thomas Leonard and Byron Larson

This book is by Thomas Leonard, the "father of personal coaching" and founder of CoachU (page 26). In his lively *The Portable Coach*, Leonard presents 28 principles to help you shape your life, career, and relationships so that they are satisfying and profitable, with 10 ways to accomplish each principle, and additional tips and self-tests. This is like having a year of sessions with this celebrated coach. *The Portable Coach* bursts with more immediately useful, personally relevant suggestions than you can possibly use. It should expand your mind, improve your performance, enhance your relationships (business and personal), help you enjoy life more, and give you many swift kicks toward becoming your best.

Rain Making: The Professional's Guide to Attracting New Clients
by Ford Harding

If you're not that comfortable with finding new clients and you're looking for a system flexible enough to accommodate different approaches, this is an extremely useful book. It is full of concrete, understated advice that you can actually put into practice, not hyped-up sales talk.

The Seven Spiritual Laws of Success: A Practical Guide to the Fulfillment of Your Dreams
by Deepak Chopra

Chopra's teachings are distilled into seven simple principles that can be applied to all elements of personal life to evoke success. The basic idea is that personal understanding and harmony promote fulfilling relationships and material abundance without extra effort: chapters tell how to achieve it.

Take Time for Your Life: A Personal Coach's Seven-Step Program for Creating the Life You Want
by Cheryl Richardson

Cheryl Richardson, former president of the International Coach Federation, offers seven-step process to switch from being stressed, unfulfilled, and overworked to "living a life you love" where you have more fun, more time, more money, and more control. Cheryl spent years as a personal coach and has put together her best insights in this inspirational, easy-to-read book.

Take Yourself to the Top: The Secrets of America's #1 Career Coach
by Laura Berman Fortgang

Laura's challenge: "If you are willing to take charge of your career like never before, if you're prepared to be responsible for the choices you make and you have the guts to have it all, then get ready to take yourself to the top."

The Truth About Work: Making a Life, Not a Living
by David Harder

David Harder presents a new vision for the 21st-century workplace, proving that traditional assumptions about the nature of work can and must change. This book teaches people how to remove the obstacles that prevent them from doing the work they love.

TOPIC INDEX

Life Coaching Programs

Academy for Coach Training, 11
Ciris Alliance, 21
Coach for Life, 24
CoachU, 26
Coach's Training Institute, 28
Coachville, 34
EduCoach, 44
Fill Your Practice, 50
International Coaching Academy, 52
Results Life Coaching, 80

Career Coaching

Career Coach Institute, 19

Parent Coaching

Parent as Coach, 74

Business/Corporate Coaching

Abundant Practice, 9
Advantage Coaching, 17
College of Executive Coaching, 36
Corporate Coaching University International, 42
Executive Coaching Academy, 48

ADD Coaching
ADD Coaching Academy, 13
Optimal Functioning Institute, 72

Spirit/Holistic Coaching
Coaching from Spirit, 32
Comprehensive Coaching U, 40
Kadmon Academy of Human Potential, 58

Relationship Coaching
Relationship Coaching Institute, 76

Coach Training for Therapists
Institute for Life Coach Training, 56
MentorCoach, 68

Life Purpose Coaching
Life on Purpose Institute, 60
Life Purpose Institute, 64
Live Your Dream, 66

About the Author

Michelle McGarry writes about hot topics in home business, careers, education, and other topics that spark her interest. Michelle began her publishing career with *The Internet Idea Book: 101 Internet Business Ideas for the Everyday Ordinary Person*. You can learn more about Michelle's books on her Web site, www.michellemedia.com. She lives in Boston, Massachusetts with her husband and their two children.

0-595-27002-6

Printed in the United States
15702LVS00005B/249